About the Author

When the author first started writing, she woke up in the middle of the night and she rose and sat at her computer desk, and, at first what she could "hear" through her mind was like a distant hymn or a song. It was somewhat like a rhythmic poem or like a verse that was sent to her through the layers of time, with this chorus... "In heaven, as in hell, we choose our actions, depending on our intent. To save, work and worry – or to trust and love – the INTENT is everything." ...and she was not a writer originally, so all this was totally unexpected. This book was given to her in her third language, and she took these notes as she wrote in a frenzy throughout four nights until it was all done.

Seven Levels of Heaven and Hell on Earth

Hille-Mia Haavisto

Book 1.

Seven Levels of Heaven and Hell on Earth

Aspects of The Universe Series

Olympia Publishers
London

www.olympiapublishers.com
OLYMPIA PAPERBACK EDITION

A CIP catalogue record for this title is
available from the British Library.

ISBN: 978-1-80074-821-7

This is a work of fiction.
Names, characters, places and incidents originate from the writer's
imagination. Any resemblance to actual persons, living or dead, is
purely coincidental.

First Published in 2023

Olympia Publishers
Tallis House
2 Tallis Street
London
EC4Y 0AB

Printed in Great Britain

Dedication

To Lukas Goguen,
My son,
-Thank You.

All proceeds will be donated to

www.lukashouse.ca

Acknowledgements

Thank you to my son,
Lukas for all joy and love in my life.

Lukas, born March 30, 1998 – died on May 15, 2017.

In the year of our Lord, 2023
Victoria B.C. Canada

Chorus: "In heaven, as in hell, we choose our actions, depending on our intent. To save, work and worry – or to trust and love – the INTENT is everything."

—

Prologue

I received this text in its entirety over the four nights between 25 September and 28 September 2012. I wrote most of it down during those four nights. My journey started then...

When I first started writing, I felt that these words were sent to me to allow You to hear what the masters conveyed. It felt like my duty on Earth. And if I resisted, I noticed that everything I did to make a living got smashed and was destroyed by those very angels who called me to bring forth light!

Life ends, but weather is an illness, an accident, war or any natural disaster that ends your struggle to be in control – these events ultimately all just emphasize in the aftermath, the sense of being, the ultimate surrender. Heaven uses this tool as a necessity to allow you to understand how much easier it is to let be, let go – surrender and let God. I have today found freedom from this seven-level structure and its power. At first, I struggled a lot, and I fell back several times on this heavenly staircase, and the heaven's demands insisted that I complete these books. Sometimes this aspect was very hard to handle, for a woman of little personal means. Thus, this book is evidently written by a force much greater than mine, something that was totally beyond my control. Read it and learn about life on Earth. Read it to understand how we impact each other, and why it seems toughest at times to seep onto the higher levels on Earth. The reasons are 'built in', but the Love prevails.

When I started to receive this text, I was still asleep.

Something woke me up at four a.m. with a small whisper that came to me as I was sleeping downstairs, a female voice that whispered – "It's time – get up"...I got up, and sleepily sat down by the keyboard and I started to hear what sounded like a rhythmic song with a four beat tempo, filtering through the layers of the universe to me. It seemed like a verse or a poem, with a repeated chorus, and it was demanding all my attention. I felt that this was like a poem delivered to me by the two grand masters: the very Archangel Gabriel, who deals with matters of love's justice on Earth, and the ancient prophet Ezekiel. A vision of purples and starry skies opened to me, and I can still see in my mind, their celestial images standing on the Milky Way, transmitting the verses of these 7 levels on Earth to me, dictating word by word how we climb via heaven and hell on Earth and always ascending toward the Love Supreme above.

Now – for the very first time in the universe – they revealed to us how this entire structure works, so that the new era of light can begin. So, this is a true story of why God created a layered structure for us here on Earth, a structure that allows our souls to ascend through the trials and personal choices toward heaven – a place our souls will seek innately, persistently, and inevitably, as they ascend toward the Love Supreme above.

Simply put: God created these levels on Earth to help our souls journey toward light.

Heaven sent me this book to explain to all humanity why we suffocate ourselves with work or fears, and why some of us are not happy. It was to explain why innocent people suffer and why God allows this. And before this, to my knowing, the entire structure of our life on Earth had not yet been revealed. Only parts of it have been known in ancient texts as a 'staircase to heaven' or the talk about a seventh heaven or the ascension of our souls, yet now it's time to get a view into the wholeness, the very architecture of the structure that we climb on our journey toward higher realms. It is all a reality, in our minds, and it is all truth received from beyond. And now we add the complete peripheral view of the levels so that you can ease out of the lower spheres and move up toward enlightenment.

This book is here to help you on your path – to where you find yourself for the first time, eternally present and being who you are, with a sense of clarity and purpose and the power of faith to achieve it. Nothing else. This structure shows you how to master a state where you can simply love, live and be. Understanding this seven-level structure on this Earth means freedom from its power over you.

To love, live and to be is our goal here on Earth.

In this book, you will also discover where you are in this structure of celestial importance. Maybe you are an achiever, working along while ignoring your soul's yearning to be. Or you may be fearing a loss of something or are in the midst of fighting a battle over money or power, and you will just need to know right now how to release yourself from this. Maybe you are even struggling with trust in the divine power? Then you need to see how to climb over this mighty mountain of fear to discover who you truly are. Or, perhaps you may have already overcome the need to achieve but are wavering between the states of love and fear, without an aim or any success in mind, yet agonizing over some wealth gathered or lost, desperately needing to know what is important and how to let go and how to have faith. Or maybe you need to understand why we chase mainstream society's idea of happiness. Is it even fulfilling? Where will you even look? And are we truly meant to struggle just to refine our souls?

One

Why Do We Suffer? Why Does God Allow It?

A thousand tears fall in the universe over those who reside in hell below level seven, the ultimate surrender to God's love toward us. The love isn't too "nice" toward us – until we choose an inner shift, and adopt a mental attitude of surrender, faith, and, ultimately, belief in God's power. But be level-headed. Don't allow others to tell you that you aren't doing the right things in life. Don't. It creates an opening for an entry into hell, and fears enter through doubt.

But test yourself often and find out where you are in this map of the aspects of the universe. This is how the love of God enters our system. We call levels one through three "hell" not because of the strife, but because of total lack of trust. And we call levels four through seven "heaven" on Earth, and beyond, because of our faith or a belief in a higher power. Fear is why we experience struggles below. Love prevails at the upper levels and guides our decisions. It is as simple as this.

To trust: this is what we are here for, to also believe so fully and completely that we move mountains with a word. "Go," we say to the mountain and it steps away. "Go," we say even louder, and the oceans part before us and heavens shift in our steps. But only if you have one hundred percent faith. To believe is essential, as we create hell over and over again when we fear and trust is built only as we reach out to Love. And IF we are open to receive communication, we shall receive it, in many forms. Small signs, omens, or even just a small thought that enters from somewhere or just like me, a tiny whisper that said: "We are here for you." But it can take a small mountain of evidence before you are ready for this. Be ready and trust yourself: trust and you shall receive thousandfold what you have invested.

Two

One Level at a Time We Climb Towards Level Seven

In heaven as in hell, we choose our actions, depending on our intent.
To save, to work and to worry, or to trust and to love.
The intent is everything.

The issue with this universe is not the complexities of life itself, or even death. It's figuring out how to live our lives here on Earth.

We know that some people are happier than others. Why? We wonder why they are happy even while suffering facing death to leave this universe behind and so on. We ask "why", yet we do not ask "how". How is it that they are content?

Nobody asks "how". But now we have a detailed explanation of how. Until now, this hasn't been explained to us and life's structure has never been revealed to anyone. However, now it's *time*. Once it's over, and the truth stands clear, we all will understand this. How this life has so much to offer. Or this: There is nothing for us to take with us to the other side.

Our life's here will all end someday – suddenly or slowly – but how we live until that ending is ESSENTIAL for our soul's ascent toward Godly realms.

This universe has three levels we can call hell. We only understand these levels and have a clear view of them **after** we have penetrated through each of them through our choices and thus move upwards to the next level.

"To be" is our ultimate purpose: an existence of trust and ease. And we can use the tool of "allowing" to ascend toward heaven, along with our breath, easing off any blame and letting go, thus developing a mindset of trust.

There are also three levels of heaven on Earth. They consist of lower heaven (level four), second-level heaven (level five), and the ultimate level on earth, level six. The seventh level is revealed to us after we die (a birth in a sense.) These seven levels form a pyramid of climbers who end up at the higher levels (or sometimes back on the lowest level for that matter) while climbing to the next set of steps toward Godly realms. It all depends on our intent.

In this life, before we die, we have many options. Choices are all ours. But before our death, some of us will achieve the sense of pure "beingness", which is the best accomplishment that we came to struggle for here on Earth.

Without support we die, or at least we wilt and wither. Without support, there isn't love or understanding of one another. Support means we care. But now we will call on Angels and hope for our salvation from this pyramid on Earth. Please read on...

Three

The Descent into Hell on Earth

In heaven as in hell, we choose our actions, depending on our intent.
To save, to work and to worry, or to trust and to love.
The intent is everything.

For most, our childhood is this Earth's heavenliest state. It is safe, sheltered as a mother's backyard and seems full of sunshine .

But interestingly, we often voluntarily choose to abandon this heaven like state and go over to hell soon after we get to the teenage years. In this first encounter of hell, we experience the more evil aspects of the universe, and we find ourselves loving achievements or lovers who aren't any good for us and who ruin our self-esteem for that matter. Here we stop making decisions for ourselves and we make ourselves suffer because we don't trust in guidance from the divine anymore. This is how we all end up ruining our best times on this paradise-like Earth: we let go of being instead of embracing it. Why do we do this? Because we are "sold" by others a state on Earth that is our own private hell. "Others are out there doing it, so why wouldn't I?" we exclaim, and most will never seek to find out who is behind all this.

Words are so powerful. There are those who keep telling

you: "You are not good enough". Or they whisper: "You aren't beautiful or handsome enough". Or they take you by the shoulders and shake you awake from a beautiful dream of childhood's bliss and ask you: "Are you successful enough? Have you got anything to show for all this? How do you compare to others? Are you ahead of the game or are you falling behind?" And so, we start to slide all the way down to the lowest levels of hell on Earth.

Four

These Seven Levels Represent Our Mental States – A Brief Introduction

In heaven as in hell, we choose our actions, depending on our intent.
To save, to work and to worry, or to trust and to love.
The intent is everything.

"A layered structure is the finest accomplishment of my love," says God, with tears in His eyes. "These layers aren't even layers; they are sentences that flow easier than rivers and the love that penetrates all layers is mine" – He vibrates. We know God exists. Yet even when we intuitively accept that He has our best life in His hand, we tend forget this: He truly loves us, and the layers evaporate without effort when His love enters our souls.

If you pray, you set start to a new cycle, a cycle of love, which ultimately releases your soul from all strife. We get released from the abyss of sadness and from all those loveless situations that are ruled by our fears. All our demons flee away, and our heart's light will shine and meet the light of those who reflect it back to ours.

There are three levels of hell on Earth. And there are three others that we can call heaven, but it depends on where we started from. I'll explain:

For example, think about smoking. For some, if they love to smoke cigars, not being able to smoke them regularly is "hell on Earth". Then again, to all those millions of people who have never smoked in their lives, it would seem rather "hellish" to have to start smoking! Thus, it all depends on where you are coming from so to speak. And, all these levels on Earth have a structure similar to these levels of "cigar smoking". The level of torture depends on where you are coming there from.

Also, these levels are not just any levels of some invisible structure that we seem to be penetrating by our choices, they are **our mental states** and the levels are layered somewhat as a pancake would be – most fluffy at the top but crusty and black at the bottom. The best part is at the top, the bottom… well, is less easy to be at.

So let's start. I am first describing all these levels briefly, as once you understand what they are, and how they work and also who is at each level, you are able to gain clarity and see what is going on in this universe.

These levels start as we enter our childhoods. Our earliest years are typically spent at the highest state. A state of pure beingness, until we fail to trust.

Our decent starts in our infancy, with our mothers or other caregivers starting to conditionalize our existence. If you are kind, you get chocolate, if you are nice, you are rewarded and if you do well in school, you are a good person. Hell starts to emerge in our soft and supple minds. As we grow up, we may wonder if we aren't about to descend even more now that trust has left our hearts.

Levels of Hell, One through Three.

The three levels of hell are generally made of fear, dissatisfaction, uneasiness, and loveless encounters with others. Jesuits would historically describe them as hell, purgatory and a state of limbo or in-between. You can never rise above "hell on Earth" if you don't allow God to take charge of your life. If we do not allow His plan to emerge, we will never truly achieve anything at all, but remain at the lower levels of hell, purgatory and in-between..

Fear dominates downstairs and it only evaporates after we are ready to let go, to let God, and to truly surrender, and after that we start to emerge toward the higher levels. For simplicity, we call these upper levels "heaven", but we also will name them in order of appearance, that is; levels four (or the first more heavenly level), level five (or the second heavenly level) and so on...

Level number One – Hell

This is the foundation, a layer of black hopeless crust made of hate, or strife over money or fame. It sits at the bottom of the universe. Soot crystallized solid. A hate without an out. Think of it as the black solid and burnt layer of the fluffiest pancake imaginable. Almost nothing penetrates this state.

Here the poor souls residing at this level are always sad, angry, and very evil and keep on seeking for solutions like escape via addictions, fights in courts and other mean things they can do to themselves or others. The issue could be hate resulting from conflict over money, or a fear that emerges with such intensity that it ruins our relationships without any hope of reconciliation. This level is truly hell on earth. Those who are here shun the other hell dwellers and can only trust life as they see it, without any trace of faith in the divine.

Only the bravest souls enter here trying to rescue these poor souls. This level is dominated by dictators, oppressed by hate troops, and here evil people massacre each other due to hate…

Level Number Two. – Purgatory

The second level isn't as bad as the first level of hell, yet hell it is, sadistic, lonely and still dark, structured to torment its inhabitants. This level is a layer of hopelessness, guilt, shame and remorse. We see ourselves as "achievers", and here all our needs are met by work. We struggle, save, sweat, and work overtime, and spend time trusting only in ourselves to "make it" in life.

This is where we have very little free time to enjoy life. We believe in nothing and think that all our "needs are met by us." This second level is some type of slow burning purgatory, where our souls will achieve oneness ONLY if we surrender and gain faith.

Level Number Three – Choices to be Made on How to Progress

At this level, you suddenly become aware of what the two lower levels of Hell consist of down below. Here you may lose all your sources of confidence, but mainly if you still seek for safety in the more material aspects of this world. You may shun

26

those who reside downstairs, yet you may still occasionally access the lower levels, if your faith, sustained now by some trust, will collapse momentarily into a heap of dusty socks and shoes, that are to be worn downstairs in hell, and even then, only when you are truly desperate. Here also fear sometimes still grabs you and shows you how some others downstairs are slowly rising upwards, each step more agonizing than the previous, desperately seeking for solace. This is perhaps a huge step for them, yet it is only a small of step for our humanity...

Rescue is found through each and every religious ritual and ceremony found on Earth. This choice is yours.

Level Number Four – Being is the Key

We have now emerged from the levels of hell on Earth with a belief in God i.e. Love as the solution for our struggles, pain and toil. And now, the uncertainty in the power of Love will become our stumble as we are emerging upwards in life.

Fighting for faith in Love is the main sensation here.

This stage also represents Heaven in that we now allow Love to lead us on our walk on Earth. If you do not feel fear any longer, how much better is your life? Is it suddenly a lot better? Is it more peaceful and contains true happiness? Or may it even become abundantly joyous?

If we still fear, at times, as majority of humanity (up to 80% of us all!) still reside underneath this solid belief-based structure of heaven on Earth, we will slide temporarily downstairs again. But this time we know how to escape it at will and many here on level four will already feel like giving up

27

all this tormenting of themselves and start to choose to believe more: Love will take care of our needs and will do so, but we do need to ask! Eventually He is to become our sole source of support.

On level four, if we trust, we fly; and if we fail, we have failed due to doubt. All fear enters via doubt, and it will often be the level two dwellers from down below that catch us here with their "advice" and their own struggles to be free. For instance, if a friend or family member or even an acquaintance isn't quite okay with our newfound states of happiness, we may feel their guilt or shame. But not even the hope of helping these others will resuscitate our state of beingness on this fourth level if we allow ourselves to be persuaded that God/Love won't be looking after us. Will you accept this now? If not, you are not yet at level four.

Level Number Five – Allow and It Shall Be Done unto You.

This state isn't easy to penetrate to… it takes a lot of faith, and a solid belief as an iron-solid defense against all evil-beings down below. There is a lot of anger outside and all fear is below, and all this evil, also known as negativity, is out there too. But here we never speak of others in a negative way, and we aren't even aware of what hate is anymore. We just hope to "Be", to become better "beings" and to "**just allow**" here. This is already nearing the ultimate heavens layer on Earth, but only if you stay solid and true in your trusting state of "being-ness" that all will be an okay at the end.

We will dwell here until we level off towards the next level,

28

where real being or – even Buddha speaks of this – the Nirvana state starts. Only true masters reach it to the next level on Earth.

Level Number Six – Servitude

This is the perfect account statement and the zero balance. We have no money left, yet we feel that we are the richest persons on this Earth. And we also know this: We penetrated by surrendering ourselves toward Love, the ultimate surrender that lifts us up beyond any hell on Earth.

The sixth level isn't hard at all anymore. It's easy. You become who you truly are, and you accept Love to be the only answer. When you finally are able to do this all your fears disappear at once.

For most of us, the ultimate situation is this. Accept "what is" and for the majority this only comes near our physical deaths. But the few who fully accept Love to be the answer way before that, will "work" here on level six for a while **serving** others. Some of the greatest spiritual masters are always at this level. They don't fear anymore, and they offer solutions to us, and they guide us – but not for any power or boost for their egos, or any monetary rewards. They offer their services and wisdom to us and only move on when they aren't needed any more, and when they die, the Heaven sings this song…

"They lived with us and left, but don't be sorry – they gave everything for us, and nor money nor fame interested them, so don't be sorry, you will see them again…"

Do you already know somebody like this?

This level is the best on Earth as nor fear nor hate can touch you here. I bet you have met at least three of these people if you are reading this book already.

Level Number Seven. Heaven Number One – For Real

This is where our struggle finally ends. After we leave Earth, we first meet all our ancestors who went before us, – and we rejoice a lot! Their Love is meeting us, and we meet our God finally face to face! The end is better if we prayed, helped others, or sought for the truth while alive, but either way, we still are in the presence of love as in a lot of light and of acceptance. Pure joy elevates us. We penetrate the veil that was hung before us when we entered here on Earth. Only one idea prevails now: How can I help others?

Five

Level One – Hell

In heaven as in hell, we choose our actions, depending on our intent.
To save, to work and to worry, or to trust and to love.
The intent is everything.

The first level, hell on earth has no sunshine at all, even if the world seems outwardly okay. This is a very lonely walk without friends and if you seek for them, they are not there for you.

This is hell on Earth. Here nothing, nor love nor fear seem real to you. This is the walk of those who struggle the most. They have not yet learned to trust:

Welcome to hell level one.

Here you tend to carry a pessimistic desire to find out who is thwarting you. You're not sure where you are in terms of trust, and you don't know if you are even liked. Fear penetrates this layer and neither your tendency to distrust nor your unhappiness in general, makes you more open to this world. The only thing that will penetrate this darkness is a jewel, a single ray of hope, where Love inserts a diamond – called forgiveness.

This is a level where we destroy others over funds or shares and where even angels tread sheltered by armies to protect their stride. "That's where you can't see us, when we are among haters," speak these Angels that are here to bring hope.

You might also turn to an army of people pursuing abuse. The accounting profession provides many services, and thousands of legal advisors rely on the advice of demons. "We'll find out who that bastard is for you and nail him!" they shout, and you smile satisfied, "They are taking care of this for me, I am SAFE finally (and the payments are on)."

Here your lifeblood drains on the fields of uncertainty over the fear of being used by somebody again. Why? Isn't anybody hearing your wails? Isn't God or somebody else supposed to be providing for all your needs? Why did everyone turn suddenly so sinister? Here you soon lose all your trust, and belief. Shame has started to erode the happiness your souls has and there is nobody you want to show your true self to anymore. This is the "solitary confinement" of hate and fear, and you feel very alone. This universe is as flat at the bottom as a pancake, over time we all seek to ascend to the top, as the easiest and most joyous states are certainly not at the bottom, now are they? No matter how hard it may be for us to realize this, we are still seeking an out – a way toward an easier existence – and attempting to elevate ourselves above the struggle and the mad rushing and climbing upon each other. All our strife to make it ceases to have appeal at the end. It's for no good, we gained nothing from it, and we aren't even satisfied. It's a steep climb upwards from here, and this may be one of the hardest things to do.

Six

Level Two – "Work Will Befree Us?"

In heaven as in hell, we choose our actions, depending on our intent.
To save, to work and to worry, or to trust and to love.
The intent is everything.

On this level we tend to save, work, and achieve. All our realistic expectations and all our needs are met by our own work here. In fact, we trust only in ourselves to "make it" in life. All while we tend to have very little free time to enjoy it all. And when we are not working, we are to be working out, while making plans to become better human beings. But if we do not find any happiness here, we become very deeply depressed, and some people plain kill themselves to escape this level of hell, or purgatory to some.

But if we could just lay down the plough, the axe and the saw, and learn how to trust, we would be freed from this level. But as they say, it takes "two to tango", us and trust in Love together, and we can only achieve oneness by accepting this truth: your needs are not met by yourself, even if you think they are, and in terms of "safety"… God wins every round! His kingdom will come, but only if we allow it to be, and *surrender*.

When we choose Love, all our pain ends without strife. All we need to do is to surrender all our needs toward the higher powers. If you now trust God instead of yourself, upwards you will ascend toward the next level on Earth.

To penetrate up to this level two wasn't easy at all, and some go into hibernation for years when they first enter here. Some may want to rest for a whole century after they elevated to here, off that pure hell down below. That hell number one, where we fought over who is winning, over money, interests, legal parcels, or partnerships gone wrong.

It's sure is hell down below, but it isn't much easier here though as work is still the center of our lives. Life is not much "harder" than before when we were fueled by anger and fear, except that now we're focused mainly on monetary achievements. With most of us having some fear and uncertainty still present, the fear-of-missing-out being one of the worst, we struggle forward day by day. As it is, both hells, levels one and two, have us strapped, snarled by the neck and keeping us very interested in the balance of our savings accounts.

Here we are still tested. Will you finally elevate your soul toward more hope via some monstrous dissatisfaction with what is? If not, neither sun nor even a gallon of moonshine can ease this pain you struggle with here on the second level.

"Choo choo!" sounds the destiny's train, "Aren't you coming aboard? I'm leaving today for Anaheim... (or any other place on Earth you love to be at.)

"Never!" you shout, "I must work! I need to work so that I can achieve. I need to work so I can be better off. I'll rest at the end."

By the way, you may find yourself at any level on Earth, at any time of any day. And your access to them is only limited to the highest level you are at. Finally, the destiny's train leaves, and we don't end up getting onboard. We return to our desks or counters or wherever it is we work. We are satisfied (and fear won this game again.) The train blasts a last puff of smoke and the train driver's hat is blown off by the wind. You catch it and say to yourself, "We aren't fools now are we – nobody just up and leaves like that." You throw off his hat and walk straight back to your parcel on Earth to cultivate.

From here you move up to the next level never by strife, but only by surrender.

But for a while it seems easier to elevate yourself above the rest with your noble work ethic. It feels righteous. You choose as you saw others choose.

"The aspects of the universe have no end, but only levels to rise up toward me," says God, as he knows that we slide back and forth between these levels depending on our intentions.

Sadly, we seldom trust His plan for us, and we will fail and of all the deaths here on Earth the saddest are those that went down without hope, or any happiness achieved, just at the brink of it all as they levelled off here, and all their trust evaporated in sand.

This pancake like structure on Earth is consisting of our mental states. This is either the fluffiest pancake there is, or a pyramid of agonizing climb in mental states, leveling off at times to nothingness. Eventually, this pancake-pyramid has the height so vast that even the most awesomely fluffy pancakes can't quite compete with it. This is simply how it's structured. It's a pyramid of Love. Seven levels high precisely.

Those living downstairs are seeking power, achievements and some other moral judgements over others and the sense of thinking: "We must do these things to achieve, to be better off than the next guy. We must always win over the competition, win a trophy, or a monetary reward. We may be the best humans, perhaps even the tallest and most handsome or the most beautiful of all people. We aren't "ordinary" beings now, are we! (Those are the others we have already won over), we are much better than them!"

This still is a level of hell as we know it. Here people punish themselves and push around, those great and small all clamper and fall and despise each other over their own failures. They aren't "evil" in the sense we typically associate with evil, and they aren't too bad either in how we usually understand the word. However, they are onto something big, – they can't seem to achieve anything without punishing themselves or others. Punishing is something they know that works. It's working for their animals: they obey. It's working at their workplaces: their employees under their command obey.

Why isn't our soul satisfied then? Why wouldn't our own soul obey if it's punished properly? And we keep punishing our own soul until it caves in, meanwhile trusting in the importance of the family honor, or working in a career that has nothing to do with who we truly are. And we aren't satisfied except when we suffer some more. The measure of success is self-denial, and we admire others while they are at it, rather than giving in to these yearnings of their souls. Now this is one of the most common aspects used to develop some type of hell on Earth. It is a very mean hell too. It is a belief-based situation, but based on somebody else's ideal of happiness, not your own.

You might follow other beliefs as well. For example, that work will set your soul into a mental state of obedience. Or that you might need a more challenging lifestyle than what you have, perhaps by jumping out of planes or skiing outside boundaries or pursuing other "hell-bent" activities that make your soul shiver! Or you numb yourself without any joy – thinking "Finally I have obedience, – I am winning over my own soul. The ultimate victory!"– or is it?

Seven

Life After All "Hell" Levels Are Done

In heaven as in hell, we choose our actions, depending on our intent.
To save, to work and to worry, or to trust and to love.
The intent is everything.

Once you start to seek situations other than money, power or others who complement your "none-ness," it's no longer hard to separate the self from the divine interventions. You struggle still, but you are interested now in the more spiritual aspects of life. At the same time, you aren't yet comfortable without a support network.

Test yourself here, allow yourself to become more used to a small intervention here and there. Treat yourself such as you would treat a friend, a friend of Love-type. A trusted friend that truly Loves you as you are. The life of the spiritual masters may interest you today, and tomorrow you believe it's a story that emphasizes all things that pure evil can't accomplish, such as devotion to a life without any "work", no excess nor any debt-taking, a life without any materialism!

Some may still get you interested in all the things you don't need, that prevent you from becoming true to yourself! These people aren't interested in your situation, and openly invite you to the brink of their disasters – be it financial, mental, or relationships, and suddenly you are there. The brink has been achieved, where are you going now?

The end seems to be here: you may be feeling suicidal as you will need to create an opening for acceptance of true joy. This joy stems from the release of all needs and wants we impose on ourselves; this joy is originating from our souls levelling to a state of pure beingness. Many can't believe this: That just acceptance of this ultimate *gift* would be the "greatest idea of all time". We call the next level three "a choice base" where a faith-based existence on Earth starts to emerge.

As we're now above the first two levels on Earth, it's easier to already think that it's all done and over with. Not so fast. We still experience clear reminiscences of hell mainly due to the other people below us. When it's truly over is after death – soon after that is, and not even then immediately. We'll talk about this more later.

Eight

Level Number Three: The "Choice-Base" Level

In heaven as in hell, we choose our actions, depending on our intent.
To save, to work and to worry, or to trust and to love.
The intent is everything.

The third level on Earth is the smallest one of them. This consists of some satisfaction, but where no happiness is achieved yet, just to boost our access to more heavenly realms above. This could be called a small scale lower-level purgatory or "limbo". Yet you may struggle with this new-found confidence as we are here to make choices about which way we want to go, and once chosen, from this level on, we are sometimes climbing better as we now have friends.

This third level is still somewhat hard to be at, but in a different way now. Our needs aren't big, and we don't argue anymore, forgiveness is also setting in...and we give up mostly everyone who still are struggling downstairs from our lives. We are now seeking to find a new way to look at life itself. And while seeking for this, sometimes uncertainty may torture you as you weren't told which way is the best one for you to climb further upwards?

But this level is also easier, and it also feels somehow different. "Easy" here is again a relative term, but we seem to just "be" a bit better here than before. To make sure we got it though, after penetrating here from the second level below without anything to rely on except Divinity, here we look at all climb-options available for us.

You may choose Jesus or Buddha as your guide, Allah's crowds struggle here also, and/or any other choices of ascent-methods or belief systems – it's all up to you here. We must make a decision though, of which path WE want to climb – and for some, this is already the first resemblance of heaven on Earth, if you like to think like that.

After this level is over, you climb on once you have a clear view of things! Sometimes we still stoop down for a bit, comparing ourselves with others for a bit, and thinking "worldly thoughts" of who has more or who has less and who is in between. There is no "out" but to leave it all behind!

But wait, a few of those who entered here still a little bit reluctantly, will want to perhaps make extra-sure that they know what hard work is all about, and may take on a re-tour downstairs. (This may last a decade even!) They will promptly slide, once this choice is re-made, back downstairs to do some more "extra" work at their perils.

There, down below, God is still in charge, and after a few futile rounds there, they once again elevate, now somewhat more easily, back to the third level, and it may also seem that they learned something new down there. For example, that things you see aren't real at all, and this: "You manifest most of them by will". Perhaps you also needed to meet "bad" down there again, to finally know this: It isn't for you after all! Or you may have needed to find a new out, where there were no other "outs" left out there...Options are many!

But as you first entered this third level, you still occasionally encounter others from level two down below. This is only natural. You will instantly know them by their struggles. Be very careful here, as these people are on the second level, and they shall freely sell you "hell on Earth", if you start to listen to them, and sometimes you think you must listen. Then you will again end up downstairs to toil some more and you may find yourself sliding straight back down to even the first level of hell. It's the blind pursuit for money that is the king down there and you may get suckered back downstairs by a false promise and a note that your services are "needed" by someone there.

As we already know, ultimately, these hells on Earth aren't a "place", they are all states of mind. So, don't keep looking back! If you do, you certainly won't make it beyond this lovely level three at all in this lifetime. Remember, you don't want to let all the others persuade you to be in their hell-bent mentalities. If you can, don't engage. But if you by accident do, you shall swiftly go back downstairs, suffer agony, feel morally alone, and have yourself pulled back there by the utter selfishness of others, their anger, and their fear-based existence that they live without love.

The purpose of this third level and the life after it, up on the more heavenly levels, is the primarily sought-after sensation of establishing love toward yourself. So, this third level of hell has to do with love of self, as well as with the love of others.

Nine

Level Number Four – First Heavenly Level
Where Being Starts

In heaven as in hell, we choose our actions, depending on our intent.
To save, to work and to worry, or to trust and to love.
The intent is everything.

At this state we begin to realize that we aren't evil beings but of Love. We start to seek the thoughts of God, Jesus, or Buddha, and we may reflect on eternity a lot. This will start our ascent. We love each other more and accept ourselves more readily. Where we still slide back and forth is in our doubts. Read on...

If you enter here at the level number four, you are already much better off than the majority below. You already have a better understanding of the meaning of what work is and also about what slavery to fear creates for us. The souls on the three lower levels, don't get a lot out of all their efforts there after all, and they needlessly spoil their situations by comparing themselves constantly with others. They thrive on the shortcomings and failures of others or even take stabs at each other for more fame or fortune for themselves down there.

Most people on this planet dwell below the third level and want absolutely nothing to do with those who are above (or those below for that matter). Life below is just "Pure Devil's

Fair" and their idea of "fun" is to get a lot of cash and to always look beautiful and thin – no matter what the price or sacrifice – that gets them there.

But it may also be hard at level four, if you still want something that you don't need or if you want someone's attention or cash. Life though, (however slowly) has the tendency to peel back these false layers, one by one, and finally the true you will emerge, and you start thinking like this: I have certain value and worth, and what I have is valuable to others.

You don't need anything from anybody else if you trust, and thus you are free from strife and all agonizing and apologizing to others who do not trust either.

This level is full of contemplation. You tend to read a lot or perhaps watch some TV (especially spiritual channels.) You take "time out". Have fun with it. "I see," you muse, as you begin to get it, and you laugh out loud maybe at anyone who isn't able to comprehend how easy it is to just Be. To truly just be yourself!

Love yourself fully! Love yourself unconditionally and with acceptance. "But what is this?" you ask yourself; here you absolutely still need to work to survive. We know, how very mundane, but the reasons are entirely different now. It is to be able to just "BE". Thus, there are no feelings of stress in this work, it is existence at a higher level, without any struggles, yet although work is just pure existence and a joy even, the tiresome effects are still felt, nevertheless.

This level may also (in some respects) be still a bit of a "hell", depending on where you come here from, but it's not as bad. And it is also more heavenly in the sense that you laugh, dance, and tend to smile and greet others a lot. But never let those below pester you again! Try not to ever end up back downstairs again, by God, this is so much better! All too tired yet still happy.

This stage is about letting go, letting be and loving yourself. Ultimately, you enter the fifth level, where you let God take care of all things. There, even work "does itself" and money flows freely, as now it means less and less to you. It is only a means to assist your basic existence and you may be dealing with the "poverty" of those from levels below. They are struggling to have what you have (without the sacrifices you made to get here!).

Don't do anything unnecessary and just enjoy! Become a national hero of "non-doing". This level is so okay. It is still "hell" in once sense – but only in all small mundane things we are to do. This level teaches us obedience, and when achieved we are freed from distilling ourselves with anger over nothing. You ultimately will just let go of it all. And when this happens, you are free to create on the next level. Although all artists aren't here, most do want to give it as much of a go as they can.

Ten

Level Number Five –
Allow, and You Shall Fly

Love isn't a state or a 'job': it's a pure state of being. Just Be, –
*and you shall receive. This is the state you see – and all else
evaporates, all else has been erased.*
This is why you came!

This is the kind of Heaven you wanted when you were on levels
of hell down below. This time, the solutions aren't provided by
parents on Earth, they are given to you from above, from
Heaven. We don't have authority figures anymore, other than
God Supreme here. But don't trust yourself to be in charge, God
is. Our only choice is this, – the choice if you "Let God" and
this choice is all yours.

Level five is very joyous, and it's sad to hear of those who
may now even criticize hell dwellers from underneath. It isn't
evil, but it is very mean, and it is just our uncertainty fighting
for faith in Love. And if we must do this, we will never
penetrate from here to the next level, also known as the ultimate
state of Love in many world religions. It is still a bit hell-like if
we stumble here, for those few who have already seen the next
level above and cannot get there. But overall, this is one the
more heaven-like levels on Earth. The Buddhists of course refer
to it still as "hell" – if they descend here from a monk-state

above! Since they used to dwell above without anything to own, now THAT is a state to aspire to …, Nirvana, that is the purest bliss on earth.

To reach the next level six, we must pray a lot and always accept all that is given and say thanks to life and enjoy what we've got here and now. Here on level five, we also thank God for this day and do so every single day.

From here you may also be sent back occasionally after penetrating through the levels of hell and entering these upper spheres, just to re-visit and to see how you lived before, and you still may even want to help others there, but it's futile. They all want to help somebody else who has "less than them," as in experiencing poverty, sickness or even death ensuing from all their abuse of self (or others), but ultimately you can't. Don't try too hard, it's all for nothing. Nobody really listens, nobody wants to be the one who has "less", but they all still want to heal through somebody else. The best help here is sometimes no help at all. Ask people to listen to you instead, and to also obey their hearts and never allow your ego boost you – that is truly the better approach. Except now, we can create this new level, being the second heavenly level on Earth but only if you choose wisely.

Here, if we never speak of others in a negative way, we stand firm. All else is equal to hope and joy, except this. This is where we truly want to Be, and to become a new kind of human being. This is so nice! To be and to allow and we have all they joy there is to be had! Here we eat, not to stay thin; we eat to enjoy food. We exercise not to get fit; we do it because we enjoy it and in doing so, we will become well. We entertain, not to achieve status in our social circles, but to gather with like souls to talk and share. We aren't about "holidaying", we just are.

And here we don't travel anymore to far away countries to prove ourselves, or to be otherwise diverted from our daily tasks; rather we gather with friends abroad to help, to meet others in faith, and to learn. Trust in it, Love yourself and Be.

If you trust in God fully, you can now just also "BE" fully and become a somewhat "God-realized person" on Earth. And if you realize this, you are far ahead of others. You already know that you will never actually die, and you know it's still a practice round here on Earth, even after the purest hell levels are over with. The level of "Being" is the measure of success here. Now FORWARD! Toward a real Nirvana level on Earth – Level Number Six.

Here we yell, "The Hell is over, we are born-again!" Or "Welcome to The Service Level!"

Eleven

The Sixth Level – Servitude (Without Any Rewards!)

This is the level to BE at. Literally. No more struggle or endless "working hours". No more loveless sexual relationships. No "others" to battle. Nobody to blame for our circumstances either. Where is the struggle now, dear ladies and gentlemen, what is going on at this sixth level of this universe, the most heaven type level we can access while alive in this body?

We have now become who we are and accept Love as the ultimate source of freedom, of happiness, and of light. The light shines upon us freely, lovingly, abundantly even. No more fears.

NOTE: NO MORE FEARS!

People here exist in a true state of harmony with each other.

This is the time to celebrate what we truly are. Love's "angels" if we want to be! We aren't at all evil, we aren't making things up either anymore. We aren't sad. "**Life**" is upon us in full force here! It is never too late for this state. The fearlessness of old people is well known. Some say it's because they don't care any longer, but that is not the same thing. It isn't nice to not care for one another, or not to care for self either! So let Love liberate you from fearing death on Earth. We have achieved the final countdown here on this planet. When you don't fear your ending, now you are free indeed!

Sometimes It's "alone is best" times here. The monk who sits in a cave for years at a time actually chose it. The love of life enters their souls. Everybody you meet here is yourself. They all are aspects of the one whole. Without knowing it, they want to let loose, learn how to allow, and how to be, but they don't just know yet what they are doing wrong. Allow – forgive – never say a harsh word, trust, and Be. Here, where silence speaks louder than words, we seek for our souls' depths. Meditation brings us to a state that isn't Nirvana, it's so much more than this. It's a state past Nirvana. It's pure unity with all that is.

This type of "aloneness" is full of light. Today, tomorrow, and yesterday, all saints used to gather in this place to save all of us others from the grips of the hell levels they left behind such a long time ago (that's their job, by the way.) Typically, the people at this state aren't easy on themselves in terms of lifestyle: no food in excess, no booze to name of. They pray a lot, and they aren't helping others for a fee, but they do it as a sacrifice towards God.

Those who penetrate all the way up to this level aren't even really "people" any longer, they are saints, sages, and masters.

Twelve

Level Number Seven or "Where the Hell Is Everybody Else?"

How you lived matters, where is irrelevant, who you met is superbly important and how you loved is essential.

The love supreme is true. Here is God and Jesus, all Angels, and Saints. Buddha, Allah – All these wise men you met... And LOVE – the ultimate being too. And all religions got it right – there is no higher Love than that you meet at this level, the level of God's total grace. This is the state you will enter after you die and all else evaporates, all else has been finally erased.

After all is done here on earth, we have a life on the "other side of the veil" where we will encounter our soul's purpose again. If we never cared to ask about our mission or the truth or anything, we aren't yet open to other situations either, this new life of a universal scale. We can enter level seven surely, but not yet eight (there are rules!), and we will get sent swiftly back to the beginning through a vast array of apologies and a noble explanation may be given and received, but never accepted by Love Supreme. We call ourselves a failure again and again, yet we will have to realize over at the far side of the universe where we are yet again – that our self-centered ways took instantly over when the "veil dropped" and how we forgot our mission here on Earth where we were sent to repent – again.

When we die, it's the ultimate let go that we experience, an ease of slipping into the oneness – where we came from – and realize Love's plan. If you struggle within at this state, your death is pain and fear, but if you find ease in you being-state already before this all, you will have ease in dying as you return to loves embrace without struggles. This leads to the ultimate sense of ease, and you are free! If you still yearn for your life's excitement during your "fastest" years however, you will see nothing, but just return to childhood moments or the lovers' embraces. These are made of timeless memories, and these moments are where the Love resided, in pure beingness, in non-doingness.

In life – if you aren't letting go voluntarily, life will make you let go by many means, it may be a terminal illness, an accident or other calamity, but the general sense is the surrender to a power larger than self. An impossible situation may come along that ends the illusion where we are the rulers of outcomes, and we surrender to its grip finally. At death, we settle all the notes – did you meet others in battle, in a state of grace or in between? Where is love in this? We answer without hesitation: up above. Now we exit off this Earth, and true bliss is upon. Everybody you meet now is Loves Being. They are all sparks of Big Love – sparks of the whole, and they will greet you in total acceptance.

Death isn't truly the end. It is a new start of an end of an end of a start. We still climb several more levels even after death, toward Love Supreme! Our end always starts a new cycle, a cycle of giving in to a better way as we seek to Love even better than we did before. The seven levels that ensue are written about in the sequel to this book – in this series of "Aspects of The Universe". When we are alone and are about to leave this Earth, we have only Love there and it has simply one function now, to decide where we go next. If we are to return to Earth to finish these steps, or stay in Heaven for real, and complete our journey there, but at the end, Love will give us all the "time" we need here. By dying momentarily we just penetrated to learn "acceptance of what is". This truly explains why some people have a "wise soul." They have been "around the bend" a few cycles already!

When we "die" we finish a job – that's all!

Thirteen –
The Aftermath

When saints and sages die, we need not be sorry at all, since when they die, they go to Heaven just to have a break, then they can enter level six once (or twice or ten times or one thousand times) more, to teach us how to live life of ease and do it right! Before your eyes…"

The rest of us can circulate the universe without hope if we forget where we came from or why we're here. We're here to help each other, and to seek truth, love, peace, and harmony. There, it's simple and easy. Ask who you came to meet, and God will tell you? Ask why you came and where you were supposed to go here on Earth, and it all will be shown to you. Don't hesitate to sell all your possessions if the answer requires it. Don't ask yourself why or how or even with what money: The Big Love shall provide, and it all will all be okay. We call it "the task" that must be done. Although others aren't doing their part, it doesn't mean you shouldn't do yours.

And if you choose to do heaven a favor while here on Earth, you shall receive rewards. Not necessarily monetary, but an apartment may be provided and a bank account that never truly runs out – if you don't spend over your daily needs! But if you do break the promise to heaven about how and who and where, then you will be stressed to the maximum and fear starts seeping in. When you need help along the way, just ask for it. It will be available to you.

Anyone who isn't willing to ask for help, is not "allowed" to use other available means as our soul needs to bend itself to do this. Also, if you cheat and hire somebody else to do all your tasks, you aren't taking on <u>Your</u> sacred tasks as God intended to, nor taking good care of your soul's mission here on Earth. And they aren't easy on you after the task is over, those "helpers" you hire or force your daily tasks upon, such as saving the world from disasters or writing books about Love or healing the sick or whatever it may be. If you truly only engage in your situation by immersing yourself entirely into fear-based money hoarding games, you will at the end, end up losing it all. Guaranteed. Then you shall die within a reasonable amount of time, and you will be sent over to Heaven's doors and sent back once more and this circle will loop back all over again.

"Try again!", it says on the small note that you may be hoarding under your sleeve when you descend back onto Earth. And the less you "try" in general, the more energy you save and the more you enjoy yourself as you are living your life's purpose and you will be better off and life is so much more easy. But if you do not follow your life's purpose and mission, you will suffer from a never-ending circle of blame, misunderstandings, possible death by substance abuse, and all kinds of avoidance techniques that leave you drained, dissatisfied and also uninterested in life's most joyous moments – such as sharing food with each other, making friends, or taking time for yourself to sleep, rest, read, sing or enjoy your hobbies, or even making others happy by telling jokes and so forth. If you aren't satisfied with yourself now, stop talking about it and do something!

Fourteen

All That Stuff You Hate to Leave Behind, When You Have to Leave It All Behind

In heaven, they don't take dissatisfaction lightly! If you aren't happy with how you look, then they may punish you by making you live in a hell of a circus of payments and scheduled appointments with the "beauty industry" as it's called over in the first level of hell, where people can't seem to be satisfied with their outer appearance. If you lose weight, gain weight or aren't exercising or enjoying yourself, it's up-to-you stuff. God doesn't deal with life's up-to-you stuff. Or, it's "Payback time."

When you enter heaven for the first time, perhaps dissatisfied with how it ended down below, they gently show you how you lived on Earth. Did you hurt somebody? Did you ask for favors and never pay them back? Did you know how many years you talked about yourself and never listened to others? Or do you take care of yourself, and never mentioned to anyone your pain? If your life sucks, it's up to you to change it.

Now, will you think again if you are sent swiftly back to Earth? This time, will you use yourself for the common good, be trustworthy, be honest, have a say in your situation? Which route will you choose this time around? Does this sound familiar? You're a repeat if you see this behavior in yourself.

Fifteen

With No Doubts We Flourish and Learn How to Fly!

The reason that all was pure hell earlier isn't because of the evil of all humans, it's also because of feelings of shame, mistrust, and the loveless struggles of those who fear. The fear dominates. Fear rules. All our fears negate our reasons to Love, to be understood and to listen to others.

For some people, others are just a source of wealth, a source to exploit to affect their own situation toward an optimistic and abundant future. All else is perceived to be truly limited. These people don't believe that those souls could be abundant simultaneously with them, even without any less or more, without any limits, and when all is evenly shared, and superbly abundant, allowing is the note we need to talk to!

The "note" here means a truly harmonious understanding and care of each other.

Brotherhood is the key toward evolution, sisterhood the key toward a society of less stress and struggles for women who would now share abundantly. The loss of the elderly as a resource of childcare and their wisdom can't be replaced. The industrial revolution smashed families and mainly exploited women.

There have been so many deaths in the furious pursuit of riches or "abundance" at the cost of others. This is the prime error of humans. Nobody wins, nobody. The exploiter creates his own lonesome misery, the exploited gets trampled to death by others who rely on their labors to produce abundance. Those in the "middle" (such as service people) have limited lives of struggle. Stress kills these people in hoards. Our society isn't abundant because we can't trust that it is.

Sixteen

We Clean Our Slates and Move outside Our Comfort Zones

Life on this planet is surely interesting enough to keep our souls occupied as though we were watching a play in a small theater. The play is titled "Universe Calls – Do We Answer?" If we do answer, we will achieve wealth without effort and seem to be free from "work" as we know it forever. If we don't, we are doomed. It's all about purpose.

The "theater" of our soul's path has a playlist of characters that aren't always the nicest people on Earth. To overcome these so-called obstacles is the first task, when we are proving to ourselves where we went wrong. Then we can think about the things that we have – that don't matter – AND THEN we are free to use ourselves, our physical bodies, toward our journey to God and that's when we are onto something special!

The journey that took us so long to complete would have taken ONLY one minute or less if we allowed and trusted more straight off the bat! Thus, the real issue isn't if we are able to journey toward God, it is whether we will fail in trusting. The faith part is crucial, and belief will follow it.

Once you trust, you can't fail if you truly are onto something this large. A true God is watching over you. Imagine for a second, if a God is watching over you at all times 24-7, what could possibly go wrong?

Trust is the key. If you trust in God, you will be okay, you truly will. If you believe with all your heart that there is a power greater than yours, you won't let anything distract you on your path and if you have faith, it's already done. It's done in a way that resembles a miracle. "Have faith," He says. The path becomes level, and all the work is done without effort, easily, effortlessly and without struggle. The End.

Seventeen

Love Is the Supreme Imperfection Eraser

The initial state of being in Love is the imperfection eraser mode. It's nesting and being in this moment. It's the ultimate time on this Earth. Yet it, too, evaporates, as strife will enter.

This time has to be preserved into our memory, as those photo albums fade. The initial time is a GIFT that we cherish, commemorate, and celebrate! At this time, we dance, laugh, hug, jump into bed together and enjoy! We are childlike. We trust. The unconditional wave of acceptance has entered our state of Being. And the openness of the other's arms resembles the unconditional love offered by a parent in the love-filled household where we lived as infants. Acceptance penetrates our soul. We open up! We expose ourselves and we laugh at our faults. We smile a lot, and we finally have joy in our hearts. Life smiles upon us and our needs are met (although we may notice we haven't eaten in a day and a half). Those who live in this state over a long period of time are ultimately the luckiest people here on Earth.

The enlightened crowd is in this state also, and only to emerge on occasion to do their tax returns! But inside, they still are in love – without the significant other – but with the beloved that is Buddha or Krishna or Jesus or the Universe.

Central to this state is the joyousness of beingness and having our needs met without strife. All things flow easily and effortlessly and when we think of tomorrow, it's full of hope.

Eighteen

Marriages That Won't Last,
or Children of Wealth

Those unions that generate wealth as a vehicle to its ultimate state of being are evil. They gain abundance, but nearly never joy. Happiness eludes this state. Just wealth, not abundance, gives happiness for these people who hoard their love to fulfill their nasty desires. For manipulating and scheming they receive nothing but aloneness, even when they are together in a union. These people support no one: they're full of evil.

"We need a trophy wife," they say, or a husband to be the vehicle to wealth, they speak to themselves, or to seem normal, they create a game – I'm better than you are – ha ha ha. But a trophy will only support our situation if we give it what it wants. A trophy isn't a husband or a wife, only an aspect of evil where things matter the most and a house is never a home for two people who love each other. A trophy husband or wife is an affliction, a tumor that grows on our energy and resources.

Marriages that aren't evil aren't perfect by any means. They can still be battlegrounds for sameness. But interestingly, they can last. There is support – the support of love, trust, faith, and hope. What else do you need? Maybe love needs no one, but all we need is love.

Nineteen

Chameleons of This Universe: Or Why Do People Want to Become like Each Other?

Many of us are chameleons: we can't shake our fears and so we blend into the background as a chameleon would. Chameleons change their color in times of fear – when they are about to be eaten alive. Fear spurs us also to blend in.

The chameleon's lifestyle is all about surviving, about blending in so masterfully you aren't seen at all. You surround yourself with the mall, with TV, with the arms of a lover and there you find shelter. You blend in with the background of the ordinary.

We see this with our youth, who don't reveal their souls to their peers. They blend into the mass marketed illusion of safety. The powerful fear response is triggered just as their lives are opening and blooming. The instrument of this torment is this: Advertising and all media shelter those who are behind the scenes but target the vulnerable, the insecure. They tell us that if we do this, purchase this or become that, we will be attractive to all those others who may even love us if we perfect ourselves according to their standards. If you love yourself, you are free of this. But most of us aren't there yet, so read on…

Twenty

Why We Aren't in Heaven
Before We Die off This Earth!

LOVE above will make you let go by many means. Whether it is a sickness, an accident, war, or natural disaster, it all emphasizes the sense of being. If we resist, some tools may be used on us, to allow us to finally understand how easy it is to let be, let go and let God or Love do its will. Control is evil! None of us controls anything anyhow.

When people attempt to control each other, we fail. We see it every day on TV, hear it on the news or social media. We learn of a sudden disaster somewhere, or an illness nobody saw coming. It's all to emphasize the aspect of the universe that we so often don't understand until we have to: the "being-ness" of our souls. Letting be is the key here. So, why do we suffer as disasters strike? It's simple: to allow us to let go of our sense of control, to let go of thousands of needs we don't necessarily have or to finally seek Heaven or the divine as The Answer to our predicaments instead of ourselves.

Life will become much easier, more effortless, when we stop attempting to have the money, achievements or love affairs that once dominated our existence on Earth as the final solution to ourselves.

By dying we complete our task of letting go of all control. If you die "fast" it gives you a chance to accept an "unacceptable" situation fast, as in ending up in an accident. If we pass away slowly, it's sometimes hard to accept it, but we chose our soul's development strategy prior to entry to this Earth. To accept pain or a disability and death as a result is the most agonizing situation we could put ourselves through to make our souls deal with some of its issues. We also teach others by being the "ultimate picture of Hell" in their faces, as we still talk about death, acceptance, and ultimately Love Supreme. This is one of the reasons, nevertheless, none of us will usually accept that pain easily.

If children die young, the loveless mother and their actions can't be overcome in a single lifetime! And if they choose to escape their suffering via substances or any other means and ask "Why did I receive this "gift" of strife just as I happened to be having fun in life? Why isn't this happening to someone else?", they have to struggle some more.

But any mother who has lost a child is a "saint" at the end of their journeys due to the hellish pain. Truly, I did journey this path! And ultimately, no soul escapes pain, the reasons are provided from Heaven, for our benefit and sometimes also for others. The death of an animal, a loved one, or a spouse is the hardest as they can't care for our needs as a partner while we are in the midst of the "learning curves".

Most ends aren't pretty, but they can be. The departure of a beloved grandmother, for example, may be an end accepted by all – even herself – as Love dominates. That's the idea of a life well spent.

When we die, we are receiving the sense of letting go that we are after here on Earth: God Rules All That Is.

Twenty-One

Who Cares If We Fall? "Not Me," Says the Universe, We Call It "Love"

Love centers around the self and fear centers around anything else. This is how it works. Love starts within you. If you love yourself a lot, then you can love others the same way. But if you don't love yourself, it's impossible for you to truly love someone else. Love stems from within you! To love somebody means it's "over" when you see each other for the first time.

"I love you" isn't an exclamation. It's a powerful statement of truth. It's a situation where love enters the "hells" of the other and also your own and the rest is history, as they say. Any hell you may dwell in, disappears instantly. Others around us disappear also and "We" is the new "me", and "ours" is the new "mine." For some, the lesson here is, do never trust anyone to know how much you love somebody or listen to anybody's well meant "advice" – it's all from hell. They live it, satisfying their needs instead of loving somebody, often taking the "safest route" instead of risking it all.

It's over when you see somebody you love for the first time. It's over the second you lay your eyes on each other, and you know it, deep inside your soul, and you just aren't prepared for it if you still deny yourself the love of your life.

They say there is "the one". There truly is "the one", as in one person alive and well who truly is the hope, the truth, the love for you, (or two or three or four…)! And if it is true love and you lose it temporarily, you will meet again, even if it's during your last day here on Earth.

Twenty-Two

The Pettiness of Those Who
Suffer and Strife

The life of a so called "perfect person" is hard. They notice imperfections in others, and they point them out, in a subtle way, in a normal walk-talk conversation, or in arguments between spouses. They do fail a lot themselves, and this is what angers them most.

They are in the second level of hell, and they can love themselves only if their own situation is seemingly much better than yours. If you want to hate yourself, you will find yourself spending time with these poor withering people. Their joy is their accomplishments, the demons of their past are in their faces every day. Where they are, they aren't at ease if they are not seen as perfect ones without any failures or human mistakes. No flaws either.

What a scenario. It's pure hell.

Over the years they have attempted to improve us all, which creates a tormenting hell for others as they try to correct the past mistakes of their elders or further perfect the futures of the younger generations. Their own situation is in their own minds perfect, obviously, except, that in the privacy of their own life, in a perfect home, in their perfect outfits, they make love only to reflections of themselves. They lack any remorse since the only person they master a true love for is their flawless themselves. But sometimes, alone in the abyss of their sadness they cry – "Who cares?", "I did it all – but who gives me any credit! I gave it all to others – advising them on how to be pretty, how to be nice, and how to redecorate to shine. Well, they never thanked me, now did they? I am over," they sigh, "Nobody cares about ME…"

A lot of these types surround us. Avoid their weird thought modalities. They tend to depress others by sucking out their energy so that they can shine. And they love to criticize, blame, and especially they love to make you doubt yourself.

These evil beings could be anyone, they may be your parents, siblings or spouses and we typically Love to please them, always, and for evermore.

But why do we please them? Why do we like them at all? We convince ourselves that they want the best for us, that they really just have our best interest at heart. Right?

We may think that they love us, yet if even a small grain of self-love could enter their misery in their existence, they would never again "love" like they did or try to work to "improve" YOU. As their deep hatred for their own selves runs more than a thousand miles down to hell, their darkness tends to abound and purely swallow us. Their loveless states are so vast and deep and furiously, very interestingly, they want YOU to fulfill all their dreams.

Twenty-Three

A Prayer for a Thousand Things

Money doesn't make you secure or accomplish anything at all. But many people mask their insecurities behind a pure hell of things. They work double time to gain something new, and they never rest.

Thing-lovers are hoarders in disguise. They love to gather a big nest of things. To not collect something is inconceivable to their indispensable collections of happiness, symbols of hope or tokens of fearless activities in the wild outdoors. They plant seeds instead of rooted plants so they can get "more" tomorrow!

And IF they haven't got enough storage; their things are asking to be organized twenty-four-seven. This takes time to make it happen. It takes all day to keep their things organized, over and over again.

As these people pass on, their things stay behind, reminding their offspring of their activities and their worth. A pile of junk to be tossed out. Things stare at us, demanding our presence. They get in the way of our lives, replacing true love and also all love for ourselves as we see just beauty that is reflected back to our souls from these things.

Twenty-Four
A Prayer for True Love

Everything seems to be about "Love" – with movies, shows and advice from others who tell us to "get someone fast". This suffocates our deep need to love for real by offering us the cheapest of advice that true love doesn't matter or that it's available and accessible everywhere. No, it isn't! Love is rare. Love is patient, love is kind. It does not envy, it does not boast, it is not proud.

The love of God is there for us as we need it. The love of another here on Earth is the force that keeps the world going around. The love of a mother is the purest of these all, as it needs nothing and gives everything, suffers it all or even dies for her child's sake.

The love of God's is there to heal our souls. And there's something specific about it.

This love is available at all times 24/7. It never fails to Love. And this Love still dies all around the world today, next Wednesday, and Friday too, and during this upcoming weekend. It is in the death of a small baby who starves to death, in death of that lonely man living alone on the streets, and in the death of a soldier who isn't a killer at all, but a kid! Love somebody today – for real.

Twenty-Five

My Love Isn't True, Until I Love You More Than I Think of Myself

Typically, we are interested in others ONLY if we gain a benefit. But when we are interested in others, not for a personal gain or benefit, we are ahead by one step. If we are interested in others by the purity of faith, we aren't ahead, or beneath, we are above those who aren't in faith. Faith adds a dimension to our devotion, and this is a situation to aspire toward. If we truly love, we aren't likely to *benefit* from any of the actions we do for the sake of others but if we aren't true, we muster there may still be a small benefit to ourselves at the end.

And if we need something, we just ask Heaven for it, and we shall receive. Only if we aren't certain, and we lack faith, then we shall fall and smell the musty underbelly of faith, all righteousness, and no action.

Twenty-Six

All Lessons That We Learned

When we are in heaven, or in hell here on Earth, we still suffer a lot. Even the most seasoned heavenly-level dweller here is suffering and will need help in any adjustment periods. We aren't perfect any of us, by any means, and we struggle as we have to ascend from one level and to the next.

So be gentle with yourselves, be very nice to one another. Be mainly sweet, gentle, nice, and kindhearted. Let's all abandon our coolness and smugness. We can create a better Earth – or heaven so to speak – amongst ourselves here.

Thus, we could be as in heaven, feeling more freedom, not stress, not experiencing worry or strife anymore. But before we can create this state, it's crucial to let go by Heaven's means.

Twenty-Seven

The Life upon Earth is Over

The death of a soul is a huge event worth celebrating! They clear themselves of all issues they came to work on. Their strife has now truly ended, and their souls proceed toward the life on the other side of this veil that we hung between us and Heaven when we entered our mortal bodies. This veil is thick, yet at the same time it is easy to penetrate, soft and malleable. Dreams penetrate this material easily, and some gurus learn to "ascend" through it at will, meditating, chanting, and working toward expanded states without any drugs.

The veil in itself is interesting. It takes on a quality of an invisible material, but at the same time it's not penetrable by those who aren't seeking God, Love, the Supreme Being.

Work is the ultimate tool here on Earth, how we manage ourselves, but after we die, our only work centers on our soul's passages or the remainders of it. The departed souls can complete their tasks by assisting others here on Earth to reach their ultimate states.

When we die, it takes but an instant, an inhalation, an exhale.

Done.

Epilogue: Opening a Box of Chocolates

The levels? There aren't any, they are all mindsets. There aren't any levels in the universe.
  You only created these to structure your thoughts.

Whatever we utter, we make true. If you realize this, you surrender more easily, you allow more freely. If you believe in all these suggestions, we say to you, "good for you". Your life eases off now to become an existence of a happy person, free from struggle! Of course, difficulties will arise, but you face them effortlessly, learning while you go through them how to take it. Just one moment, one breath at a time. The love we have for others grows by deeds done for those who suffer more than ourselves. The love for ourselves grows as we treat each other with the same respect as we treat ourselves. We sow kindness and reap gratitude. We make love and issue notes of affirmation that we truly are interested in all you speak about, always listening and being there for our loved ones. Now – I am not done here, or did you want to quit?

Is this perhaps all I just made-up by allowing my mind, often less than brilliant, to play around with all things sacred? No, it isn't. This was given to me and I merely sat down to write it all up. As some kind of "Gods Note Taker" only. I have mostly no idea what I am doing in life myself, so it is certainly not ousted from my brain. But I took more than ten years to write this all down. This is my work here on Earth.

I truly hope this will bring you as much peace and joy on Earth that I have received from this knowledge! We all want to be happy, and to know and understand what these levels are, will free you from its grip!

That's what these levels stand for. And now, finally, the universe gives you here again all the keys you need to unlock these levels on your climb towards heaven on Earth and beyond!

You're welcome!

Keys for Moving Through the Layers

The only way we progress through the levels up toward God is through our choices. We can't leave any level and proceed upwards, until we accept that we need these keys. Any key is a choice of our free will. Once you accept it, you will surrender and float to the next level above, but only by *that choice* we choose to make by our very selves.

In level one – the pure Hell on Earth – the fight over money is a bloody battle for certainty or victory. **Forgiveness** is the key to unlock this level of hell, and forgiving someone is the **only** way out of this pure hell.

This structure here just supports our egos. We win, we lose, we have, we have not. The ego is the reason many people struggle and even end up sending others to desolate states to elevate themselves alone! To rest is impossible unless you are "above", winning some battle of your choice. Reasoning is not an option either, since you forgave nothing, and your hurt is upon their lives. One or the other wins, the rest is left behind and only the victorious smiles, but only for a while.

But we can't achieve anything by trampling those below. Nothing is achieved and nothing gained. To arrive at the second level, winning is never an option. Never! To rest below isn't either. That's why it's pure hell.

"Forgive, and you shall be free," say Heaven's angels. Forgive yourself first for trying and then forgive others for their deeds as well, and you shall elevate easily to the second level.

In level two – the purgatory of self-achievements – the poor souls think that tomorrow they shall free themselves from all worry. They never rest and they satisfy their needs by doing so much, and even more needs always to be done. In this level of hell there is no rest. People here say, "I can never quit my job or be satisfied, I will overwork myself, put in all the overtime I can, over many years, over millions of dollars, over there, somewhere in the city of no returns."

But the "God wins every turn" rule stands. Life isn't about, achievements, or bank accounts. Surrendering to love is the only way out. **Surrender** to the flow of life. If you don't, you struggle through all eternity and will never be free for fun and laughter, for jumping into a haystack with a lover, or for any free form delivery of happiness from above. Jump in, and Let Go. That's what we came for… not to work or build up savings accounts. "I take care of thee," says God, smiling at our laughter over the happy times we had while here. He sent us, his children, to play, to discover and to Love.

Level three is the layer of **choices**. Here we are seeking for answers and how to choose love over fears. We allow if we are brave, we wither if we fear. Our egos still boost our efforts to stay in control and steers our ways back into some hell on Earth below. **Choices** what way to ascend will be ours, at the end of the day, but how about this – let go of the steering wheel and allow. Trust, faith, and happiness all go hand in hand, if you believe there is a God above who watches over us. He sees your strife and He also sees the lifestyle we lead, and why you cry at night. But the allure of control all is huge! Take this counter-intuitive gift and turn it right side up – trust first, take a leap of faith, and then you shall believe when you see it at work. How about this for a change?

In level four, we stand without a note – no money or anything else to hold dear. All is taken, given the rest. Here it is. All of it. We allow The God we believe in, who sits in heaven and watches us, to lead our every-day existence. He isn't interested in our satisfaction or our struggle to be famous or rich. He wants us to think differently, think more freely, think globally, and think green, even. Just be a lot and consume less, become an elevated form of yourself as you let go of everything – and everything shall be okay. Must we think of monetary issues or bank accounts? Is life only a mere numbers game? What if bank accounts suddenly burst open with millions due to your gifts and money flowed in as freely as birds flock to water. What if? This situation takes two to master: you and Heavens help together. **Be** and you shall move up to the level above without a worry or sorrow, and love will take care of it all. There still are voices that berate us and tell us all kinds of loveless lies, but don't listen to them! Only evil monsters take charge, but angels just guide. Be, and you shall sleep well. Have faith and you shall soar. We promise you Heaven on Earth if you, my dearest child, let go of the "work" you have and follow the lead of your heart.

In level five, by already knowing how to Be, we proceed to a more significant reunion with God-Above. We think we can handle most aspects of the universe, but we cannot master anything without guides, angels and spirits who know the patterns we weave with the threads of our lives here on Earth. Their beauty is astonishing by the way! **Allowing** masters to direct us and allowing our thread to weave our own true colors, we emerge from within. **Allow and seek not** anymore, this is the reason we came. Here we may feel alone, even bare to the bones, and behold, we could master it all IF we learn to just allow…

Thus, forward to the next level and toward all that love can create. Listen to your soul speak to you about love and a fearless existence, guided by guides, masters and Love Himself; believe this, you have support. Believe it and you will succeed again and again.

Level six is the closest we get to real Heaven here on Earth, and again we seek for nothing. **Service** is key and the tool here. If we are still seeking for something, we tend to slide down at times. Only **non-seeking** satisfies. Together we pray, to all our saints, *"Please be with me today."* And yet, nothing really is to be done and at the same time everything is done perfectly. This is the best level on Earth. It's called sages, saints, and Angels, who rotate to get here over and over for reasons unknown. **Service is the key** and without their help we would likely never make it here, as we need examples for our souls. We need them to know how to "Be" up in here, near our souls 'roots' or seats, the aspects of it all, but are all understood now.

In level seven: we die and penetrate to Heavens levels above. We leave our Earth-suits, and nobody can be excepted from this path, and here no pesky thoughts here to enter to pester our existence anymore. We flow or float, together in all that is. We are also finished now with our tests, and we can't go "wrong" any longer, this really is heavenly in that sense!

This Love realm is surreal together with somewhat surrealistic to us at first. Everyone is so happy and elated, and joy is above us waiting for us all. We hope you enter here to greet Joseph and Mary, Allah's fantastic crowd, and all the millions of others you Love... All angels greet and wave back, "Hey, can't you be good?" Today it's all over, but it begins at the same time. We are all together again (everyone you lost too) in this situation we call the seventh level. So surreal and yet so real! And anyone who needs a "repeat" of levels, is soon sent back after they take a short break, a thousand years or so, or more, and others continue on. This heaven has levels also, seven to be precise, but more to these in the next volume of this book series...Aspects of The Universe. And to you over there, who may sit there still holding doubts, guess what? Here those who stay for good are into an orientation and then "work" – it is heavenly "service" again and these souls work to help others still down in Earths levels. (That's why some seem to "see ghosts" of their departed loved ones soon after they departed!). But after their "work" is done here they elevate to the second heavenly realm and so on. To learn how love differently, and finally to experience the ultimate surrender – becoming one with Love.

We still can choose to rotate fast to Earth again, perhaps if you so wish? Some just rest first, to get free from any pain from Earth-times and getting used to this stage of freedom in heaven, the first true upstairs "mode" we see after we die. This is a situation where when you just trust in faith you can carry over without fears. **Acceptance** is key here.

But if trust in all things "not too nice," then, even after you die, you can still experience them – maybe on Earth, maybe here, or who knows, who even cares! – but better yet, you get to try over and over again until you truly get it. Only Love makes the universe go around.

To be is the purpose of life, to live is the joy we get and to love is the blessing we all should embrace.